Molly, by Golly!

The Legend of Molly Williams, America's First Female Firefighter

Dianne Ochiltree

Illustrated by
Kathleen Kemly

CALKINS CREEK
AN IMPRINT OF ASTRA BOOKS FOR YOUNG READERS
New York

For information about permission to reproduce selections from this book,
please contact permissions@astrapublishinghouse.com

Calkins Creek
An imprint of Astra Books for Young Readers,
a division of Astra Publishing House
astrapublishinghouse.com
Printed in China

ISBN: 978-1-59078-721-2

Library of Congress Control Number: 2012933452

First edition

10 9 8 7 6

Designed by Tim Gillner
Text set in Caxton Light
The illustrations are done in oil paint on
gesso-sealed watercolor paper.

For the strong, brave women in my life
—*DO*

For Lisa T.
—*KK*

"**O**ur Molly is as fine a cook as any in New York City,"
the lads of Fire Company No. 11 liked to boast.
"In fact, she's wondrous fine!"

"Molly's hasty pudding is tastiest," the Captain always said.

"No sir," Isaac would declare, "it's her chicken roly-poly makes a man's
mouth water."

"Hot apple tansey is Molly's most delicious dish," Jonas was sure to insist.

The argument would go around the fire company's table until the very last
bite of venison stew or codfish muddle had disappeared. But on one thing,
the men agreed: Molly, by golly, put hands and heart to every task, in or out
of the kitchen.

One wintry day, she proved just how wondrous fine she could be!

Inside the cozy kitchen of Mr. Aymar's house, Molly Williams briskly whisked cornmeal, eggs, and buttermilk in an earthenware bowl. Outside, snowflakes swirled thick as cream. Snowdrifts stood tall as haystacks. Molly stirred glowing embers in the hearth oven . . . and worried.

As the johnnycakes baked, a fierce wind knocked at the door and whistled through chinks in the red-bricked walls. Molly worried more. Snow covered the neighborhood that morning, and a terrible sickness had spread like a thick blanket over scores of households. Influenza! Many of the volunteer firefighters were already sick. Even Mr. Aymar lay abed with it.

Molly scratched the upturned chin of Eliza, one of her many household cats, and wondered aloud, "If a blaze sparks in a blizzard such as this, what will our poor fire lads do?"

Molly recognized a sound growing louder above the whine of the snowstorm. Had her worry about fire come true?

Church bells *clang-clang-clanged*. They sang out a fire alarm! The number of times they chimed told Molly just where the trouble was. "Something's afire, Eliza . . . and it's nearby!" she exclaimed. Molly wrapped a heavy woolen shawl around her shoulders and dashed out to spread the news.

Molly spied a small knot of neighborhood boys speeding
toward her with lanterns held high. Runners! Molly, by golly,
led them through snow-filled alleyways and icy cobblestone
streets. The runners rattled clackers and rang muffin bells.
"Fire!" they all cried. "Come out, come out!"

Men burst from their homes with bootstraps flapping and coattails flying. Women and children tossed out leather water buckets. Molly and the runners scooped them up as they raced to the fire company's equipment shed.

Volunteers busily loaded axes, pull-down hooks, and coils of rope into the fire wagon. Molly took a quick count. She'd never seen so few men answer a call!

The Captain lifted the buckets from her aching arms. "Molly, by golly," he said, "you're always ready to lend a hand."

These hands can do much more than bake johnnycakes, she thought. She clapped a weathered leather helmet on her head, strapped spatterdashes over her woolen leggings, and pulled on heavy work gloves. "Wait for me!" she cried.

"Molly, by golly!" exclaimed the surprised Captain. He waved her over to the line of men struggling to drag the heavy pumper engine into the snowy street. Molly took her place on the rope and gripped it hard.

"All heave-ho, lads . . . and lady," the Captain ordered. "Get this pumper on its way!"

"One, two, three, PULL," they chanted.

Molly and the men rolled the pumper engine straightaway into the street.

They dragged it through swiftly drifting snow. Wintry wind whipped at Molly's face and hands, but she never lost her grip!

Soon Molly saw ribbons of soot twirling between snowflakes. She heard frightened voices floating through the frozen air. Then there it was: a small wooden house, ablaze.

"Step lively, now!" cried the Captain through his tin speaker's trumpet. "Fire wagon and pumper to the side yard. Volunteers and buckets to the river!"

Close to the snowy bank, the Captain chopped holes in thick ice. Jonas and Isaac dropped buckets into the frigid water flowing below. Molly and the others formed a bucket brigade, passing water hand to hand, filling the tank fast.

"Start pumping, and be quick about it!" the Captain shouted.

Molly jumped to join the men at the pumper engine's sides.
They cranked the heavy, long pump handles until water gushed
in a steady stream from the fire hose.

Hour after hour . . .

Molly sprayed burning timber. Angry flames hissed and spit each
time water hit them. Molly pulled down chunks of burning roof with
a hooked iron rod. Flaming shingles melted the snow the moment
they hit the ground. Choking smoke crept into Molly's nose. Cinders
clung to her woolen shawl. A wall of heat warmed her cheeks.

My fire lads won't let this fire win . . . and neither will I, she thought.

The fire raged and roared with the fury of a wild bobcat . . .
until at last . . . it was out.

The Van Horn family shivered in their snowy yard. A haze of
smoke surrounded them. They were thankful to be alive—glad
the fire had not spread throughout the neighborhood.

Bone tired, Molly took her place on the drag rope to pull the
pumper back to the shed. Jonas, Isaac, and the other volunteers
rushed to her side, broad smiles on their soot-covered faces.
"Hooray for our new company volunteer!" they cheered.

"Molly, by golly, you're as fine a fire lad as any," added the
Captain. "In fact, you're wondrous fine!"

AUTHOR'S NOTE ABOUT THE RESEARCH

I first "met" Molly Williams years ago when I was researching firefighting methods for another historical-fiction manuscript I was writing. The text simply mentioned her as "the first known female firefighter in America." Having been a little girl who wanted to drive a fire truck, I immediately set out to learn more. Gradually, additional bits and pieces of information about Molly, and the legend for which she was known, surfaced in books on the history of firefighting. My respect for Molly Williams's courage, strength, and heroic volunteerism grew with each retelling I found. So did my determination to bring her legend to life for young readers. My retelling fills out the original tale with historically accurate depictions of the era's firefighting techniques and equipment. It's my hope that Molly Williams's story will inspire young people who dream of one day becoming firefighters.

FREQUENTLY ASKED QUESTIONS

What is known about Molly Williams?

Very few details are known about her life. Molly was an African American woman living in New York City in the early 1800s. She was a servant of a Mr. Aymar, who was said to be a member of his district's volunteer fire company, the Oceanus Engine Company No. 11. It is believed that she wore a bright blue calico dress and checkered apron wherever she went.

Molly distinguished herself when her neighborhood volunteer fire company desperately needed her help during a blinding snowstorm. With courage and determination, she helped the small group of struggling volunteers drag a heavy pumper engine through the snow. The fire was eventually extinguished, thanks to her help.

Molly's bravery earned her the undying gratitude of the fire company men, along with the nickname she proudly carried for the rest of her life: Volunteer No. 11. Thereafter, she worked tirelessly alongside the men to battle blazes at any time of day or in any type of weather.

Why didn't Molly cook at the firehouse?

Fire companies in the early 1800s were run by citizen volunteers, and "fire engines" were hand-pulled water-pumping carts. There were no firehouses. Instead, neighborhood fire companies had wooden storage sheds with small fenced yards. Since Mr. Aymar was supposedly an engine-company volunteer, Molly probably served as cook for both her employer and his fellow firefighters.

Most meals would have been delivered from Molly's kitchen to the fire company's equipment shed for the men to eat at business meetings or social events. In good weather, she might have cooked food outside over a campfire. Some accounts say that Molly took johnnycakes and ham slices, wrapped in linen cloth, for hungry volunteers to eat when fighting a fire late into the night.

Why did Molly run through the streets to let her neighbors know there was a fire?

In Molly's day, there were no alarm boxes or mechanical sirens to call volunteer firefighters to duty. Instead, the companies had a group of young volunteers called "runners." These boys ran through the streets yelling and making noise with handheld bells and rattles. Churches had big, loud tower bells—every neighborhood had at least one—so these were used to warn people of a fire as well. The number of gongs or the pattern of notes acted as a code to give the runners, and everyone else, a rough idea of where the fire was burning.

Why did Molly and the men have to fill the pumper engine with water from the river?

Early pumper engines had to be dragged by hand to the scene of a fire. If a pumper engine's tank was already filled with water, it would be much too heavy to pull through streets at a reasonable speed. Firefighters would be tired before they even battled the blaze. So they filled it once they reached the fire.

Water might be drawn from a well or a cistern, but the most reliable and plentiful source of water came from a nearby river, lake, or pond. Each citizen was required to provide at least one bucket for firefighters to use in a brigade line to fill a pumper or throw directly on flames. Neighbors often tossed out the buckets to the runners as they went by.

Have more questions about firefighting, yesterday or today? There are lots of places to look for answers.

BOOKS

For Primary-Grade Readers

Gregory, Helen. *A Firefighter's Day*. Mankato, MN: Capstone Press, 2012.

    Kids learn what firefighters do to keep people safe and how they do it.

Royston, Angela. *Fire Fighter!* New York: DK Children, 2011.

    Follows firefighters as they respond to an alarm and battle a blaze.

For Middle-Grade Readers

Gorrell, Gena K. *Catching Fire: The Story of Firefighting*. Plattsburgh, NY: Tundra Books of Northern New York, 1999.

    Covers the history of firefighting techniques, training, and apparatus as well as modern-day methods. Includes information on fire prevention, first aid for fire injuries, and the simple physics of fire.

Masoff, Joy. *Fire!* Principal photography by Jack Resnicki and Barry D. Smith. New York: Scholastic Reference, 1998.

    Excellent overview of the historical developments in firefighting as well as innovations developed in modern times.

Reeves, Diane Lindsey. *Virtual Apprentice: Firefighter*. New York: Chelsea House, 2008.

    Behind-the-scenes look at professionals in the field of fire safety. Includes information on modern firefighting techniques, tools, and training.

Thompson, Lisa. *Battling Blazes: Have You Got What It Takes to Be a Firefighter?* Minneapolis: Compass Point Books, 2008.

    Helps young people understand what it's like to be a firefighter. Uses photos of on-the-job events as illustration.

WEBSITES*

    Many sources of information about firefighting are on the Internet. Here are a few that may be of special interest to kids, parents, teachers, and librarians.

Keeping Kids Safe from Fires. usfa.fema.gov/prevention/outreach/children.html

    The U.S. Fire Administration (USFA) reviews and collects resources for parents, teachers, and other caregivers to explore fire safety with kids.

Let's Have Fun with Fire Safety. usfa.fema.gov/downloads/pdf/publications/lets_have_fun_with_fire_safety.pdf

    The USFA also offers a free, downloadable 16-page activity booklet for kids.

National Junior Firefighter Program. juniors.nvfc.org

    Sponsored by the National Volunteer Fire Council for boys and girls.

Only You Can Prevent Wildfires. SmokeyBear.com

    Smokey Bear and friends are featured in games that teach kids how they can prevent forest fires. Link to campfire-safety resources for teachers and parents.

Sparky the Fire Dog. sparky.org

    Sponsored by the National Fire Protection Association. Kid-friendly fun and games about fire prevention and safety.

*Websites active at time of publication

MORE FIREFIGHTING LINKS*

African American Firefighter Museum. aaffmuseum.org

International Association of Black Professional Fire Fighters. iabpff.org

International Association of Women in Fire & Emergency Services. i-women.org

PLACES TO VISIT

Many cities, large and small, have fire museums where you can find out about the history of firefighting, see firefighting equipment and uniforms from the past, learn fire-safety rules . . . and have *fun* at the same time.

To find a fire museum near you, check out the Fire Museum Network's directory at firemuseumnetwork.org/directory.* You may also want to look for this special guidebook in your local library: *Discovering America's Fire Museums*, edited by W. Fred Conway, published by Fire Buff House, New Albany, Indiana.

SELECTED BIBLIOGRAPHY

Coe, Andrew, and the New York City Fire Museum. *F.D.N.Y.: An Illustrated History of the Fire Department of the City of New York*. New York: Odyssey Publications, 2003.

Costello, Augustine E. *Birth of the Bravest: A History of the New York Fire Departments from 1609 to 1887*. New York: Tom Doherty Associates, 2002. Abridged text of title below.

Costello, Augustine E. *Our Firemen: A History of the New York Fire Departments, Volunteer and Paid, from 1609 to 1887*. New York: Knickerbocker Press, 1997. First published in 1887.

Dannett, Sylvia G. L. *Profiles of Negro Womanhood*. Vol. 1, 1619–1900. Yonkers, NY: Educational Heritage, 1964.

Ditzel, Paul C. *Fire Engines, Firefighters: The Men, Equipment, and Machines from Colonial Days to the Present*. New York: Bonanza Books, 1976. Distributed by Crown Publishers, 1984.

Golway, Terry. *So Others Might Live: A History of New York's Bravest; The FDNY from 1700 to the Present*. New York: Basic Books, 2002.

Gottschalk, Jack. *Firefighting*. New York: DK Publishing, 2002.

Kenlon, John. *Fires and Fire-Fighters: A History of Modern Fire-Fighting with a Review of Its Development from Earliest Times*. New York: George H. Doran, 1913.

Kernan, J. Frank. *Reminiscences of the Old Fire Laddies and Volunteer Fire Departments of New York and Brooklyn, Together with a Complete History of the Paid Departments of Both Cities*. New York: M. Crane, 1885.

Masters, Robert V. *Pictorial History of Fire Fighting: Going to Blazes*. New York: Castle Books, 1967.

Ryan, Keith. *The Illustrated History of Fire Engines*. Edison, NJ: Chartwell Books, 1998.

Smith, Dennis. *Dennis Smith's History of Firefighting in America: 300 Years of Courage*. New York: Dial Press, 1978.

Wagner, Rob Leicester. *Fire Engines*. New York: MetroBooks, 1996.

Wallington, Neil. *Firefighting: Heroes of Fire and Rescue Through History and Around the World*. London: Anness Publishing, 2005.

Wallington, Neil. *The World Encyclopedia of Fire Engines and Firefighting*. London: Anness Publishing, 2004.

ACKNOWLEDGMENTS

I'd like to thank David Lewis, curator of the Aurora Regional Fire Museum, Aurora, Illinois, who generously contributed his technical knowledge of historical firefighting tools and techniques throughout the writing of this manuscript. My gratitude also goes to Damon Campagna, director and curator of the New York City Fire Museum, for his insightful comments about Molly's story, as well as to writer friends for their thoughtful critiques. I thank my family, as always, for their patience, understanding, and support as I researched, wrote, and revised the manuscript. I am indebted to my illustrator, Kathleen Kemly, for bringing these words to life. My deep appreciation goes to my editor, Carolyn P. Yoder, as she skillfully guided the book to completion with the utmost care. Last, but not least, my thanks to all firefighters, volunteer and paid, who routinely risk their own lives to save the lives of others. You're an inspiration to us all!